Digital Skills Series. Short read Book 5.
Adaptivity and flexibility and Tools and Techniques How to develop it.

Copyright © 2019 by Digital Studio Management.

Book and Cover design by Digital Studio Management.

What you'll find in this book?

This book is for all kind of leaders, managers and employees who understand inevitability **of digital change** in a business environment and therefore would like to be essentially prepared for it. This book is for all those that wants to live educated and well-prepared, in a current so-called Digital Ages.

This book covers content of adaptivity and flexibility two **of crucial skills** necessary for leaders who want to change their company into a digital enterprise and need therefore appropriate knowledge base.

In this book you'll find:

- Suggestions of useful **tools and techniques** how to strengthen digital skills that hopefully help you to lead your company through digital change also called: "digital transformation",
- Summary which you can use as a **reference of necessary actions (or checklist)** to increase your digital literacy and that can be introduced in your company and also:
- List of **useful books** and **web pages** you can use for further comprehension.

We hope that this book will be useful for your digital literacy skill development–if so, let us know: digital@digitalstudiomanagement.com.

Table of content

Digital Age

In this book we will frequently use a term of Digital Age therefore it is worth to start with some definitions what does it mean?

Digital Age (with its synonyms of: Information Age, Computer Age and New Media Age)[1] is associated with historic period in the 21st century characterized with an economy based on information technology. This is a period of shift made from traditional industry that the Industrial Revolution brought through industrialization, to current, informational-based times when data and its transformation into information places a particular role.

Digital Age is the period when digital industry shapes a knowledge-based society surrounded by a high-tech global economy. It is a time when people use technology and digital means of communication both in everyday activities and for a business purpose.

We will use "**Digital Age**" in capital letters to underline its essential role in the business environment which is made by information and technology use.

As means of Digital Age we will in particular understand: new digital products, new digital channels and new social media that occurred in 21st century. Digital Age boost a use of digital devices and electronic media both for private and business purpose. We face huge change in the way we communicate and also—behave.

---

[1]   By Wikipedia:
      https://en.wikipedia.org/wiki/Information_Age

Digital Leader and digital transformation in the organization

In this book we use frequently term: "Digital Leader". It is worth to clarify that by this term we won't mean only those that hold (or plan to hold) title of Chief Digital Officer, Head of Digital or any other similar name of the position. By "Digital Leader" we mean a person who truly leads digital change in his/her company, despite of name of his/her position. He (or she) is in fact a leader and moreover the one who believes that implementation of digital practices is necessary for a further company's development.

We mark **"Digital Leader"** with uppercase to emphasize the difference and importance of leaders, who takes an active role in disruptive change which **brings digital transformation** to the company.

Digital Leader is the one that should have necessary knowledge on how to benefit out of the technology in an organization. It means that she or he knows **which technology** can be used and **how to use it**, for better performance of a company. Knowledge of possible digital impact on business is useful on every step of digital transformation. Digital Leaders is the person who should find a way of proper digital transformation.

Digital transformation is an essential change made in the organization to implement means necessary in Digital Age environment like: digital devices, appliances, use of digital channels and data transformation for the benefit of business goals.

To make successful digital transformation change

Digital Leader has to wisely and cautiously answer questions like:

1. What is the best technology tool or tools for my organization to perform, business strategy and gain market success?
2. How will this technology help employees to serve our customers?
3. Which are best practices (use cases) of use of a particular technology tool?
4. Which are the most important technology tools we need in our company?
5. What technology tools will improve a company's ability to perform business strategy and gain market success?
6. What technology would improve the way our company is communicating with our customers, potential customers, stakeholders and employees?
7. Has the company all necessary resources to get, perform and share information efficiently?
8. Is the company able to use technology in secured way? Have employees enough knowledge to revise trustworthiness of information used for making business decisions and many more, regarding use of digital tools, devices and practices.

Luckily (for him or her) it does not mean that Digital Leader is alone in looking for those answers. There are other leaders which are his or her natural ally in this journey. For example CIO[2]. Some of above-mentioned questions on a possible technology to be introduced in company, might look like natural competency of CIO, as he or she runs technology in the company. Or they might look like shared competency with CIO's or IT manager agenda.

---

[2]   Chief Information Officer – person holding highest position for Information Technology responsibility area

It has to be remembered that **Digital Leader has cross-functional competencies**, and IT is one among them.

It is worth to underline that digital change is an exceptional duty of Digital Leader. It's not also a duty of CIO or CTO whose role and duties differs and are more connected with running the technology. Or as one may say: "keep the wheels on" meaning ensuring that all elements of technology work well and changes applicable to them goes without a hitch. But it's Digital Leader's role to find out if for example: Company is missing tool for better data queries that could increase potential sales. Final choice of a specific tool compliant with a corporate technology stack should be in hands of CIO but a definition of a business case belongs to Digital Leader.

The same comes with social media appearance. It is most likely in hands of marketing to decide about the specific messages content company is spreading. But still it is up to Digital Leader to rise a hand and say that company is missing efficient tool for information sharing or the information should be shared through digital media and target customers over electronic channels.

Definition of adaptivity and flexibility skills

> *"Let no one think that flexibility and a predisposition to compromise is a sign of weakness or a sell-out."*–Paul Kagame

According to Wikipedia definition: "Adaptive behavior refers to behavior that enables a person (most frequent used in the context of children) to get along in his or her environment with greatest success and least conflict with others."

Adaptivity however do not only refer to children. Also as a grown person we have to adjust ourselves and our behavior to the conditions served by environment. Therefore adaptability is an important skill as it helps to adjust oneself behavior to changes in its actual place to live or work (f. e. workplace). This skill helps to decrease a stress resulted by changed conditions.

Both adaptivity and flexibility skills are enables for an easier **reaction to change**. As a rule the reaction to change that has taken place in our environment but also in a wider definition, to changes in other people's behavior.

The difference that brings Digital Age is a necessary speed of adoption that is higher than ever was before. We don't have generations or even years to adopt. Today's adoption has to take no more than days and sometimes hours. Being adaptive and flexible is a must when creating and living in a digital workplace.

What is adaptivity management?

As with every skill and behavior we can learn it and practice it. Constant development of one's reaction to change supported by essential monitoring of environment conditions is known as adaptivity management.

Following definition given by Wikipedia: "***Adaptive management*** *(AM), also known as an adaptive resource management (ARM) or adaptive environmental assessment and management (AEAM), is a structured, iterative process of robust decision making in the face of uncertainty, with an aim to reducing uncertainty over time via system monitoring.*"[3]

Effective adaptive management requires both careful monitoring of the resource side of the enterprise and available information flows both from inside and outside of the company.

Adaptive process requires a step-by-step changes application so that management of resources or style of enterprise management gets adjusted to various changes. By doing this iteratively uncertainty of the environment gets recognized and adaptation process can start.

Adaptation is not a short run process. As with every process of learning its outcomes may appear in mid- or long run. This makes it even more difficult to utilize in comparison with pressure given by necessity of short term achievements.

What is the difference between adaptation and flexibility?

Adaptivity and flexibility are both about ones respond to changing circumstances and expectations.

Flexibility[4] is being "willing or ready to yield to the influence of others; not invincibly rigid or obstinate; tractable; manageable; ductile; easy and compliant;

---

3   https://en.m.wikipedia.org/wiki/Adaptive_management

4   https://en.wiktionary.org/wiki/flexible

wavering."

As it was said before, adaptivity skill enables step-by-step change made within organization so it can, in mid or long run adjust to its environment. On contrary, flexibility refers more to quick reaction for rapid (and usually unpredictable) situation.

Adaptation means that step by step we follow the change and as a result of external change our behavior changes as well.

Flexibility does not change our interior. Flexibility is rather a reaction we express to adjust to a sudden situation.

Flexibility means we are as an organization somehow **prepared for an unexpected situation** but not necessary adjust to them our behavior. We can react but we don't change ourselves.

Being "flexible" means that besides of my plans and agreed schedule, I am able to compensate sudden changes made by circumstances both made by other people (delay or delivering too quickly) or by environment: changes in numbers of orders, changes in customer's behaviors and habits, changes in competitors set up.

By Forbes[5], adaptability provides a foundation for change. It is not only about changing a course or approach but to make it with smoothness and timeliness.

---

[5] https://www.forbes.com/sites/jeffboss/2016/04/26/staying-competitive-requires-adaptability/

Why adaptivity and flexibility is an important skill?

Current world is unpredictable and fast-changing. Even the best strategy has to possess a space for changes if (or as soon as) external or internal conditions or prerequisites change. Changes in the industry can disrupt the status-quo like: new communication channels with customers, impact of social media on traditional businesses or new ways of resource planning like: cloud computing and use of robotics and artificial intelligence. All those changes causes problems even for biggest.

In its report Right Management [6] highlights the growing importance of adaptability in business. 91% of HR decision-makers believing that people will be hired based on their ability to deal with change.

Leader cannot be rigid and unwilling to be proactive. Being resistant to ongoing changes will condemn his or her business to the dust as the whole world moves on. He or she may even not notice that world has change and his (her) business is fallen apart. Unwillingness to change and rejection of adaptation is a slow death of the business.

---

[6] https://digitalmarketinginstitute.com/en-ca/blog/03-04-18-the-most-in-demand-skills-in-digital-leadership

How to use adaptivity skill in Digital Transformation

What's the role of Digital Leader in modern Digital Age to let his (her) business survive?

First of all, he or she has to be able to:
1. **Perceive** a change in an internal condition or external environment.

Being blind for changes delays process of adaptation. We do not see the change so, we cannot adopt our company's behavior. To see the change is therefore a first step to any change. To be able to see requires preparing up front important to our business condition we would like to track. Only by having them in our minds but also stated in written and known to people in organization, we shall be able to perceive a change.

2. **Estimate its impact** on agreed strategy or defined projects.

Naturally not every change has the same impact on our business. Most likely there are few important changes that will have an impact like: a new aggressive on the market competitor or totally new model of customer servicing. Therefore competitors or newcomers to the market should be on the top of your list but do not underestimate changes coming from technology market. Companies that used to be IT companies might come competitors for banks, insurance companies or media market. Having a technology is a powerful tool. Watch biggest on technology market to know if they can enter your market and with what an offer.

3.   Define necessary changes.

Once you find out change is happening on the market, it's time to prepare for it. First question is whether the company should react flexibly and not to change its long term market behavior. Or maybe it's time to adapt to change and let change ourselves? At this point of a time analysis of possible scenarios should be made. On the base of this analysis further decision of priority projects and changes is essential.

4.   Communicate and integrate it in an overall plan.

Change won't happen if nobody knows it. Moreover, people are keener to take a part in the change when they understand the purpose of it. Therefore absolutely important thing is to inform people in the organization on: what has been found in the business surrounding of the company? What impact it might have on the company? And what is a company's answer to these changes, and more precisely what is a plan of change?

All those four-step actions has to be done regularly, so a company is prepared at any point of the time to adjust to changed conditions of the environment. Also, scenario-based analysis can be made regularly, even before any change is noticed.

"Collaborating, learning and adapting (CLA) is a concept related to the operationalizing of adaptive management in international development that describes a specific way of designing, implementing, adapting and evaluating programs"[7]. Collaboration is

---

[7]   Akhtar, P., Tse, M., Khan, Z. and Rao-Nicholson, R. *Data-driven and adaptive leadership contributing to the sustainability of global agri-food supply chains connected with emerging markets*, International Journal of Production Economics, 181. pp. 392-401.

one of crucial skills, as much of adaptation learning process requires collaborative, group work. Through interaction with others, new idea and solutions arise easier and in more adequate way. We will come back to this skill development in further part of this book.

Enhancing collaboration is not only important for people in the organization. The importance of collaboration is closely linked to the ability of organizations to collectively learn from each other. Organizations that has this ability are commonly named by "learning organization"[8].

Therefore supporting people in the organization to work as a team, enhances also company's chances to successfully cooperate with other companies on the market as part of chain or network.

(2016) , ISSN 0925-5273, http://eprints.uwe.ac.uk/27723.

[8] Garvin, David A. *Building a learning organization.* Harvard Business Review 71, August 1993, no. 4: 78–91.

Tools and techniques to improve adaptive skills

1. Use a power of data

Uncertainty is simply saying: lack of data and information made out of data. This causes lack of reaction or lack of proper answer to changes coming from (usually external) world. Something you don't understand happens and you either do not notice it or do not understand it or – that also happens – underestimate its impact. All those happen due to lack of data.

One of best ways to harness this issue is simply support yourself with as much information from outside of your company's environment. To understand data coming from outside, you have to be equipped with data describing your own company. Only by comparison (benchmarking) you'll know whether you are lacking behind the market and to what extent.

Partially uncertainty might be a sign that not enough weight was attached to information before.

Several steps can (and should be) done to work it out:

Try to describe your business with as much metrics as possible. It can be customer side and preferences. It could be cost side and most likely key processes that take place in the company.

1. **Gather data** on metrics you choose for your company. Let's build a model of your company but described by numbers not by words.
2. Try to get as much **market benchmarks** for metrics of your company as possible.
3. Comparing metrics and process data of your company with those from **benchmarks** you'll

find differences and deviations.

4. Look into them deeper. What are the **reasons of abbreviations**? Is it resource pool what limits your business? Or maybe there is a new market opportunity that has not be elaborated before?

5. What data and information gathered from market tells you about the **change in the environment**? Does this picture put a light on the uncertainty which appeared?

6. With a use of computer, build a model of your company and analyze what can and should be done as a result of knowledge gathered from the market.

7. **Analyze alternatives and possible change** to so far taken strategy or strategic directions. Is should be a natural adjustment of business and financial goals but in the light of sudden change in the environment this action takes on validity and importance.

8. Once several alternatives are calculated and described, gather all people in the organization that might help to **evaluate alternatives** to choose preferred one.

9. Discuss alternatives and changes. Prioritize them. Estimate them by feasibility and by time and other resources necessary to its implementation.

10. **Apply necessity changes (adapt) or react flexible.** Uncertainty might by both threat and opportunity, Take a chance on the second option.

2. Observe Changes In The Environment

To have enough time to adjust to changes in the business environment, it is essential to have a list of cases, measures and circumstances to be monitored. All those parameters and prerequisites that were taken under consideration when business strategy was defined or important decision on further direction of business was made. This will make it easier to carefully check if any of those parameters have been changed.

As soon as list of monitored is prepared, **regular routin**e of its monitoring should be placed.

It is worth to assign it as somebody's duty or make it personally.

If no regular habit and a routine is implemented, monitoring of conditions and measures gathering would be fragmented and therefore inefficient. If this will happen, the company will react with a delay and - most likely changes applied would have to be bigger and more difficult to introduce. All those together might undermine effort since the world will not wait for those that lag behind. In result company will miss its chance to adapt and react on time.

When adaptivity fails?

As it was said—first step to change adaption is having appropriate information. Reliable information should always be based on data. Do not believe and most of all— do not relay on information made by: "people's saying", "common knowledge" and so on, since most likely you'll let yourself to base on more or less adequate gossips.

Always, always rely on data. **Reliable data**.

However there are several reasons for which adaptive management based on data might not succeed[9].

This has to be remember so not to copy it.

First of all data collection is never completely implemented. Measures are defined but a number of it makes it difficult to collect all of them and therefore analysis do not deliver essential results.

Second reason is when data are collected but not analyzed. Effort given to data collection is wasted by a lack of power, willingness or just time to analyze it.

Third reason occurs when data are analyzed but results are inconclusive. There are many reasons for which this situation might happen. Sometimes it is due to improper measures choice. Sometimes measures are properly describing company but a situation in the environment changes that quickly that analysis does not show any specific trends that can be utilized. This situation requires continuous monitoring as potentially the situation might change in any direction and clarity.

Fourth situation is when data are analyzed and are interesting, but are not presented to decision makers. It might happen that situation that clarifies from data seems so awkward, misunderstand or simply against analyst's personal attitude and beliefs that he (she) will not present them for decision-makers. It might happen also that attitude and company's culture do not support such information sharing as being against management's belief. Therefore it is crucial to set up adequate corporate attitude so anyone in the organization is not afraid to present even most inconvenient data and information.

Finally fifth situation occurs when data are analyzed and presented, but are not used for decision-making because of internal or external factors. Well, possible

---

9   L, Elzinga, Caryl; W, Salzer, Daniel; W, Willoughby, John,. *Measuring & Monitoring Plant Populations*. U.S. Bureau of Land Management Papers, 1998-01-01.

the worst situation. This might mean that company lost its ability to adjust to customer and market expectations what means that soon will fade away in the market. It's a matter of time when also financial data will show that situation is bad. It's final time for implement rapid changes to adjust to changing market conditions.

3.   Enhance collaboration

As it was already mentioned, collaboration is necessary for efficient adjustment process.

Leaders has to have ability, skills and willingness to empower employees to make their own decisions. That requires a high level of self-awareness and others awareness'. Leader setting up team must understand everyone's skills and abilities, as well as limitations and reserves.

There are many evidences and - I believe personal experiences as well - on the importance of collaboration among individuals and groups. It refers in particular to processes which concerns innovation, creation of new products and processes, knowledge management and transition of various forms of information. When staff is interacting with one another and sharing knowledge, new (and better) ideas comes and final solution is tuned through many brains.

> To enhance collaboration manager has to constantly actively **work on stimulating group work** instead of individual's achievements.

He or she has to support knowledge exchange and assign time slots when people can freely work in self-set up teams. When teaming is not (yet) a part of an organizational culture.

Digital Leader is the one that encourages team members to perform best possible cooperation and helps to resolve issues which might occur and diminish the effort.

Therefore it is up to the Leader to make sure that team has necessary tools like: internal social network to exchange ideas, portal to visualize work products or videoconference systems to make remote members work as one team despite geographical distance.

Especially the last one, meaning how to work efficiently in virtual teams might be a challenge. All team members have to learn how to show empathy in more difficult, remote environment. One has to learn how to explain complex matters when in-person contact is exchanged with videoconferencing connection. They also have to learn how to have a personal touch while they are miles away from each other. These are challenges of remote teams which are so current in digital organizations.

> People has to possess the **right and will to self-organize** and share products of groups work as they appear.

People are in majority social and tent to work together if only circumstances, like managers or discouraging corporate culture do not indispose them.

Close collaboration of teams requires frequent exchange of ideas, thoughts and sometimes a discussion on a specific subject. Teams itself more and more often are build-up with members who have specific skills and abilities. As it was mentioned, more and more often they are unnecessary work in the same place and cooperate as one virtual team.

Generally leader's role is let people self-organize. However if things do not go in good direction or goes there too slow, he or she should assign necessary time, place and attention. What is also important is that it is Leader's role to widely show his or her appreciation for groups and team achievements.

If you do not know where to start with and how to ignite such kind of close collaboration, set up a formal appointment as for any other meeting. In the agenda of such a meeting put a specific task or challenge to be resolved, so team members called for the meeting can elaborate as a team.

Leave a team **freedom to self-organize** a way of work on given assignment.

Another good way to increase collaborative work is a self-example of Leader. Leader should show that his or her idea come from group's work and team's exchange of idea.

4.   Develop a culture that values flexibility

This technique is probably the most difficult to implement in full extent. But to the same extent is the most important one.

Having **an organizational culture that values flexibility and quick adaptation** to both internal and external changes is a huge advantage and change enabler.

If you feel you don't have currently such an environment in your company means hard work to achieve it. Therefore if things will not go as quick as you might expect, don't feel defeated. Change of the organizational culture takes approximately 3 to 5 years or even longer. Usually it takes much longer than strategy change, what has to be remembered when strategic planning is performed.

Anyway, every change starts with first steps. If you won't ignite them, they will not happen for sure.

Flexibility and **change acceptance** should be one of major values of the organization and this should be expresses in any possible way.

This enables change acceptance in a workplace and

easier adoption to any situation. Part of this culture should be a flexible approach how to conceive the digital workplace.

To introduce flexible culture, first of all it is worth to check if coworkers have any ideas on how to do that. Most likely there is knowledge (or at least strong will and idea) how to handle this situation within a company but hides waiting for encourage to speak it loud and realize.

It is also worth to make an enquiry on how would flexibility help the workplace and how would it benefit for customer service or product delivery.

By asking people in the organization about their idea on implementation of a flexible environment you'll get two important things:

True engagement in the change, as this is going to be "their" idea, not a command from manager(s);

You gather collaborative knowledge on what's the most important to change and how to do that. Usually if more than one person is performing a plan, it is going to be more insightful and thoughtful.

After a first punch of ideas is a gather, choose those areas when achieving flexibility would be the easiest. It is so called: "low hanging fruits". Those that you can grab easiest and–more important–the quickest. The purpose of that is to have first changes as soon as possible to encourage further progress. It might be marketing area or research and development team, when flexibility culture will start its presence. Mentioned areas are those that usually take a leading role in any change therefore using this as a sandbox for changes is a good trial but you have to find out what will work for your company the best.

One more advice. New product development is the most important part of organization where flexibility culture should be implemented as soon as. Changes to products are those most expected by customers and usually delivers best results, both in terms of visibility of change and in true financial outcomes.

5.   Actively work on change acceptance

You have to remember that changes will happen whenever you accept it or not. They will come whenever you are prepared for them or not. Changes are the only content thing in our lives. Therefore it is worth to develop a positive attitude toward them.

Positive thinking and openness to changes will help much to manage them. We cannot predict the future. But we can prepare for changes before they will happen. You cannot adapt to unknown expectations but you can develop flexibility skill so that when they occur, you can easily react.

People have a natural resistance for the change therefore good idea is to prepare yourself and them for the inevitable. Change will happen, question is only which and when. Leader should be open for new ideas happening in the surrounding. Whenever they occur and whatever impact they will have, it will be easier for him or her to take necessary action if his or her attitude toward them will be possible.

Prepare yourself for the change. Train your reaction for change by recalling situation when you were in a similar one and how you managed to solve it.

Once you prepare yourself, share it with people. Let them know that you are prepared and so should they be.

This will give you the courage to face and implement changes as they occur or even before they occur.

6.   Be ready for a quick change of execution

Every strategy or even every decision made is based on certain prerequisites for which a given direction seems to be valid. In particular those that describe expected behavior of market, competitors and customers. Therefore monitoring of the business environment is one of significant elements to trace adequately the change and–if necessary–change taken approach. It is worth to note important prerequisites that makes your strategy valid and put into practice to control it over the time.

Development of this skill is a composition of:

- Information seeking,
- Analysis making skills,
- Ability to find an optimal solution,
- Ability to test a plan but most of all,
- To leave the fear and not to be afraid of the change.

The better you feel prepared mentally, the easier you take what circumstances will bring. Therefore circle: "Search ->Analyze->Choose an optimal solution->Test it->Roll it out" has to be constantly in practice.

Leader must be ready to make quick-fire decisions to keep company on track with minimal negative impact. Even the best pre-agreed approach may not be adequate if condition change. So, as a Leader, be prepared to change, to adjust and a proper communicate it.

7.   Avoid procrastination

Leaders shouldn't let changes to pass-on-by. They have to take appropriate action at an appropriate time without unnecessary delay.

The earlier action is taken, the better effect will bring. Leaders should have in mind that the same changes are happening to their competitors and the one that adjust a course quicker wins.

There are several various ways to avoid procrastination. One of them is to plan carefully what has to be done by what time. Regular monitoring of due actions helps to protect from slipping It is said that any (good and bed) habit can be omitted (or introduces) during a 30-days long a new practice training period. Announce then (to yourself or maybe for others as well) "a month with a delay". Put yourself a rigor of an instant: decision making. As it was mentioned already several times, Digital Ages differs from previous times by speed. Even worse decision could be better than a good one done with a delay. Worlds has changing constantly and so should we. Therefore to not delay, do not put off for other time any important action.

8.   Adjust your Leader's behavior to situation

As said by Brittney Anderson: "*Leaders need to recognize situations in which their old behaviors are not working*"[10]. Effective leaders are active seekers of new solutions or new leadership paths (see more from our book series: "*Intellectual Curiosity...*"[11]).

In broader scale leader should adopt his or her style to different employees' expectations. Changes the way he or she behaves might cause inspiration on people's behavior and embrace change adoption to the organization. Many people are not keen to change. We naturally connect change with discomfort. It is human. It is within us and there is no point to deny or fight it.

It can (and should be) changed by proper actions. Changing leader's attitude is the first step and make

---

[10]   http://www.sigmaassessmentsystems.com/flexible-leader/

[11]   Digital Studio Management, *INTELLECTUAL CURIOSITY and Tools and Techniques How to Develop it*.: Digital Skills Series. Short Read: BOOK 4. https://www.amazon.com/gp/product/B07TKLW5FW /

people follow this path.

If you are afraid of sudden changes, you can always make a kind of "sandbox" by choosing one area when you let yourself for a change of behavior. For example if you have a tent to micromanagement and like to check if everything is okay, find one area of the company when you'll let people be more self-responsible. It can be really limited subject like: how to organize a company's cantina or it can be a bigger one like: new product introduction. It depends how comfort you feel with that change. What is important in this technique is that you train and learn to behave differently than you done before? This will learn you and your people as well not to be afraid behave differently. Once again, Digital Ages are about speed. Some habits that used to work before (like micromanagement which might be your way to make sure everything is checked and prepared in a required manner) will not work in the world of constant changes.

9.   Actively seek opportunities to be more flexible

Routine is easy to follow and proper routines are necessary for effective and consistent management. But on the other hand routine might kill adaptivity... Leaders should to put themselves in a situation when their flexibility can be extensively developed.

Imagine, what more we can do to be more flexible and ready for adoption of changes.

Let's start with basics.

Mind Tools Content Team [12] gives such four examples on how to be more flexible:

---

[12]   Mind Tools Content Team, *How to Be Flexible in the Workplace*,
https://www.mindtools.com/pages/article/flexibility-at-work.htm

- *"**Offer to help** out another team member if you notice that he or she is overloaded.*
- *Volunteer to **cover a colleague's work** while he is on leave.*
- *Consider allowing people **to work from home** to help them achieve a better work/life balance.*
- *When you come across a problem, offer up a **variety of solutions** that might fix it."*

As a manager and leader you'll have to adjust frequently your managing skills to a different kind of people you work with. People have different priorities in their life and also different attitude toward change. You have to learn it and you have to adapt to it. One size do not fit all.

The same one managing style do not fit all employees. However if you will treat people with respect, they deserve and appreciate their differences as a benefit not as a trouble to be overcome, it might happen that you'll find in those differences a new company's asset. Simply, when the change come, it might happen that those that were unsatisfied with: products, services or conditions that company offered, might be those who most actively put themselves in the change process and therefore ease company's answer to the change.

✂ --

Fast track and "to do's" for adaptivity and flexibility skill development

1.   Use a power of data

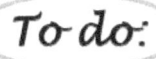

☐   Gather measures that best describes your business and your business data.

☐   Obtain benchmark values and compare to those you can see in your business.

☐   Analyze deviations and in particular reasons of them.

☐   Apply necessary changes to your business strategy and direction accordingly to seem results.

2.   Observe Changes in the Environment

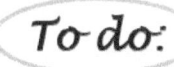

☐   Make a list of prerequisites which have been a base for decision making or strategy.

❑ Put into practice a routine to monitor if those prerequisites are still valid for taken strategy.

3. Enhance collaboration

To do:

❑ Make sure your coworkers understand an idea of co-working. Describe to them ground rules and a new way of decision-making process

❑ Enhance collaboration in the organization by assigning necessary resources like: time slots, convenient place (physical or virtual) and tools that help idea exchange.

❑ Give people the right to self-organize. Only if you see that for some reason they don't actively participate in team working, put a little effort to ignite the process by assigning time, place and rules of group work.

❑ Value and loudly appreciate ideas made as a result of collaboration work.

❑ Empower people so they can make their decision based on teamwork.

❑ Support collaboration in the organization

by self-example. Present how you come to conclusions during teamwork and exchange of ideas with others.

4. Develop the culture that values flexibility

To do:

☐ Organize enquiry on how people see flexibility in the organization. What's their opinion on how higher flexibility would benefit for organization and how to make it happen?

☐ Implement changes to discover which good market practices can be introduced in your company. Look out both in your industry and externally to it.

5. Actively Work On Change Acceptance

To do:

☐ Be prepared for the change. If change is a part of your plan, put necessary effort to plan it carefully so you will face less unexpected surprises. For changes that comes from other's be prepare to respond.

☐ Have few scenarios in mind and even better - put it in paper so you can come back to them as necessary

6. Be ready for a quick change of execution

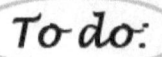

- If any of important to business market or internal prerequisites do not fulfill - be prepared for a quick change of direction.

- Good idea is to have a few possible scenario of changes up-front and in case of necessary to start them quickly.

7. Avoid Procrastination

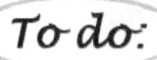

- Give yourself inner timer on how much time must it take from trigger to action and trace if you don't exceed it.

- If above task cannot be achieved by your self-discipline -ask somebody to trace it for you and keep you updated if you're on track.

8. Adjust Your Leader's Behavior Appropriately To Situation

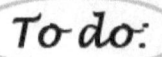

- Actively seek if the way you behave delivers positive results or simply still works for people? If not - seek for changes and adopt it,

☐ Even through you believe your behavior is still adequate - try to change yourself from time to time and check out how it works for others.

9. **Actively Seek Opportunities To Be More Flexible**

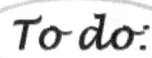

☐ Find yourself a time slot when you'll think only about what I can do for being more flexible?

☐ If you prefer to make it as a teamwork, it is fine to organize a kind of workshop but make sure you'll only focus on this topic and not for current issues.

Place for your notes and comments on what to do:

1. ....

2. ....

3. ....

4. ....

5. ....

6. ....

7. ....

8. ....

9. ....

10. ....

✂ --

Bibliography and where to find more

1.   Useful books

Clark Andy, 2nd November 2015, *Surfing Uncertainty: Prediction, Action, and the Embodied Mind*, by Oxford University Press

Conroy Michael J., Peterson James T., *Decision Making in Natural Resource Management: A Structured, Adaptive Approach*, Wiley-Blackwell; January 3, 2013

Cragun Shane, Sweetman Kate, *Reinvention: Accelerating Results in the Age of Disruption*, Greenleaf Book Group Press, July 26, 2016

Klein Gary, *Streetlights and Shadows: Searching for the Keys to Adaptive Decision Making*, A Bradford Book; September 30, 2011

Leland Fred, Vandergriff Don, *Adaptive Leadership Handbook - Law Enforcement & Security*, Adaptive Leader LLC, January 7, 2014

Cross Barry L., Brohman M. Kathryn, *Project Leadership: Creating Value with an Adaptive Project Organization* , CRC Press; 1 edition, July 1, 2014

Sanford Carol , *The Regenerative Business: Redesign Work, Cultivate Human Potential, Achieve*

Extraordinary Outcomes , Nicholas Brealey Publishing; 01 edition ,November 30, 2017

Smith Cathy C.; *How to Become a Digital Leader: A Roadmap to Success Publishing*, CreateSpace Independent Publishing Platform, 2018

Snyder Nancy Tennant, Duarte Deborah L., *Strategic Innovation: Embedding Innovation as a Core Competency in Your Organization*, Jossey-Bass; June 30, 2003

Steffine Gregory P., *Hyper: Changing the way you think about, plan, and execute business intelligence for real results, real fast!*, Sanderson Press; 2 edition (July 13, 2015)

Strock James, *Serve to Lead: 21st Century Leaders Manual*, Serve to Lead Group, 2018

Wagner Sonia, *On Working Remotely: A Guide on How to Implement Remote Work For You and Your Employees*, Amazon Digital Services LLC, April 4, 2016

2. Useful web sides

https://edwardlowe.org/striking-a-balance-in-management-flexibility-vs-rigidity/

https://ideas.ted.com/tag/leadership/

https://leaderchat.org/2017/08/24/3-ways-leaders-can-improve-their-management-flexibility/

https://papers.ssrn.com/sol3/papers.cfm?abstract_id=1098111

https://smallbusiness.chron.com/advantages-flexibility-organization-37369.html

https://www.bizjournals.com/bizjournals/how-to/growth-strategies/2014/03/4-tips-for-being-more-flexible-and-adaptable.html

https://www.mindtools.com/pages/article/flexibility-at-work.htm

https://smallbusiness.chron.com/advantages-flexibility-organization-37369.html

https://www.superception.fr/en/2018/02/05/how-to-structure-a-communications-organization-in-the-digital-age/

https://www.thebalancecareers.com/workplace-flexibility-definition-with-examples-2059699

About this book series

This book you have just finished is fifth out of 7 books in the series. We design this series to lead you through our subjective selection of 7 most needed skills essential for current times. You'll find books covering a subject of: "Digital Strategic Thinking..." (Book 1)13, "Digital Literacy..." (Book 2), 14 "Communication and Advocacy" (Book 3)15, "Intellectual Curiosity" (Book 4)16, "Adaptivity and Flexibility" (Book 5- the one you have in front of you)), "Collaboration and inclusivity over hierarchy" (Book 6) and last but possibly most important: "Customer and user-centric journey" (Book 7).

You can read all books in the series one-by-one or you can choose one of them as a stand-alone guide to a single digital skill you're interested in or the one you

---

13 Digital Studio Management, *Digital Strategic Thinking and Tools and Techniques How to Develop it.* Digital Skills Series. Short Read: BOOK 1. https://www.amazon.com/gp/product/B07RM4 PBRY/

14 Digital Studio Management, *Digital Literacy and Tools and Techniques How to Develop it.* Digital Skills Series. Short Read: BOOK 2., https://www.amazon.com/gp/product/B07RXS R7ZQ

15 Digital Studio Management, *Communication and Advocacy and Tools and Techniques How to develop it.*: Digital Skills Series. Short Read: BOOK 3, https://www.amazon.com/gp/product/B07S9Y RNF5/

16 Digital Studio Management, *INTELLECTUAL CURIOSITY and Tools and Techniques How to Develop it.*: Digital Skills Series. Short Read: BOOK 4. https://www.amazon.com/gp/product/B07TKL W5FW/

need to augment the most.

Each of the book presents single skill and an explanation why this particular competency seems to be crucial in—so called — "Digital Age". By "Digital Age" we mean current times when technology plays a key role in our life and changes the way we run businesses.

Few books in this series are available to buy, while others are under preparation.

Let us know if you'd like to be informed when they will be available. For those that send us an e-mail of interest, we'll prepare a special offer for existing books and inform as soon as a new title will come.

We intentionally made every book short, so you can read it while standing at the queue or traveling. However, short reading rarely fulfill whole content of the topic. These books also only marks out key ideas on this wide topic of digital skills. On the other hand, it will help you to recap your knowledge almost instantly.

We hope this short read might make you hungry enough for more. For those who wants to further develop one's knowledge—there is a list of books and web pages enclosed at the end of each book.

We did our best to make this book useful. If we succeeded - let us know. Also if you disagree with our thesis or have any other comments—give us your feedback through Amazon's book page or directly:

digital@digitalstudiomanagement.com.

www.ingramcontent.com/pod-product-compliance
Lightning Source LLC
Chambersburg PA
CBHW030545220526
45463CB00007B/2981